CONTENTS:

INTRODUCTION:

Hello reader and welcome.

My hope for this book:

That it helps a few golfers improve their games.

Simple. Modest, but true.

I had the idea for this book years before attempting to write it.

One of the first things I noticed as a coach, is that there is no coaching manual. I thought:

"If only we had a check list of reasons why golfers strike the ball fat. Another check list of reasons of why golfers strike the ball thin, etc. My job would be so much easier."

Drum roll please…

Well – here it is:

'Faults & Fixes'

A check list of reasons why you could be playing the shots that you are.

I started coaching in 2016.

So why wait 4 years to write the book?

I put pen to paper (or finger to keypad) and suddenly realised, the research required to write such a book, would take forever and a day. Who would ever have enough time to research and write such a thing???

Fast forward to March 2020... I'm in a National Lockdown, housebound and have a whole lot of time on my hands.

I'm convinced there will be AT LEAST ONE THING, in Faults and Fixes, that will help EVERY GOLFER who reads it.

I'm sure there will be SEVERAL THINGS, that will help MOST GOLFERS who read it.

& I hope there will be DOZENS OF THINGS, that help SOME GOLFERS who read it.

Wishing you all the best with your game,

Jak.

How to Use This Manual:

You don't have to read this manual in the 'traditional' sense, as in from cover to cover.

<u>You can skip to the chapter that is relevant to you.</u>

There are two main ways of using Faults & Fixes:

1)

AS A FAULT FINDER:

E.g.

You've just played a round of golf and hit a few shots fat. Go to the FAT CHAPTER (page 62).

Assess which aspects YOU are most likely doing. Then practice to **stop** doing them.

2)

AS A FAULT FIXER:

E.g.

You want more distance. Go to the INCREASE CLUB SPEED CHAPTER (page 169).

Assess which aspects YOU are least likely doing. Then practice to **start** doing them.

(That's the hard part... Putting in the practice **to include / exclude** them from your game)

An Alternate Way of Using Faults and Fixes:

Is to ask yourself one of two questions:

HOW or WHY:

E.g.

HOW do I make my attack angle shallower?

WHY is my attack angle shallow?

The ATTACK ANGLE SHALLOWER CHAPTER (page 142) will help answer those questions.

A Statement That Sums Up This Entire Manual:

"THERE IS SO MUCH THAT CAN GO WRONG IN GOLF.

AND YET:

THERE IS ONLY 'SO MUCH' THAT CAN GO WRONG IN GOLF.

There really is so much that can go wrong. We could miscalculate:

- Weather
- Wind
- Temperature
- The lie of the ball
- Altitude
- Changes in slope and elevation.

We won't reach our potential unless we have the proper:

- Club selection
- Course management
- Custom fitted clubs

Golf isn't just about "swinging good". There are many aspects:

- Driving
- Fairway metals
- Hybrids
- Long Irons
- Mid irons
- Short irons
- Fairway bunkers
- Pitching
- Chipping
- Greenside bunkers
- Putting

All these potential pitfalls.

And yet... (**The ethos behind 'Faults & Fixes'**):

There is:

'Only so much' that can go wrong.

Right??

I mean... There can only be **so many reasons** why a golfer keeps shanking the ball!!!

This thought process is the inspiration behind *'Faults and Fixes.'*

Asking the question: '**What are all the reasons a golfer keeps shanking the ball**?????

What Has Been Researched:

There are different types of 'bad shots' in golf.

The shot types researched in this golf coaching manual are:

1) Thin Shots
2) Fat Shots
3) Toe Strike
4) Heel Strike
5) Open Club Face
6) Closed Club Face

Not necessarily 'bad shots' but also researched in this golf coaching manual:

7) Club Path Out to In
8) Club Path In to Out
9) Attack Angle Shallower
10) Attack Angle Steeper
11) Increase Club Speed

Factors 7-11 would probably be better categorised as "swing types."

But for the purpose of consistency - all the factors will be categorised under the same title:

"SHOT TYPES"

Ranges of Movement [ROM]

Pages $28 - 52$ have researched the **club**, the **ball position** and **10 major body parts**, (*upper & lower body*) assessing each of their <u>ranges</u> <u>of</u> <u>movement</u> [ROM].

Every single range of movement, has been applied to every SHOT TYPE within Faults & Fixes.

The findings of these results is what can be seen from pages $53 - 177.$

NOTE:

Pages $28 - 52$ contain lots of technical / medical terms for the ROM.

Within pages $53 - 177$ (the Faults & Fixes) you will see simplified terminology, making Faults and Fixes more 'user friendly.'

Notes on Set Up

Faults and Fixes has been written to help you improve your full shots.

However, an outline of how to set up to the golf ball is included in this manual.

The Set Up outline can be seen on page 12.

NOTE:

The information in the Set Up chapter will move you into an orthodox position.

However, personally, I'm an avid believer of moving away from what is orthodox, if it serves your impact position more effectively.

I call this:

"<u>Optimising your Set Up</u>."

It's Not All About Having A Good Swing

Reader be aware of this:

This golf coaching manual is designed to help your long game.

There is so much more needed to reach your potential as a golfer, never neglect to work on your <u>short game</u> & <u>putting</u>.

<u>Shot shaping</u> and <u>ball flight control</u> are massive attributes.

<u>Equipment</u> can help or hinder.

<u>Course management</u> and <u>self-control</u> are to be continually enhanced.

10

Starting Point to Improvement

Before you get to work on your swing. <u>Please check your *strike*.</u> It's the most overlooked factor in players trying to improve.

When you can consistently strike the ball out the centre of the club face, learn to develop the club face *angle* (where the club face points at impact) - it's largely responsible for the launch direction of the ball.

Once these two factors are repeatable, work on *club path*, which is largely responsible for the curvature on the ball.

That would be my 3-part, place to start, recipe for improvement:

Strike, Face Angle, Club Path… "When these 3 aspects are under good control, your ball flight will be too."

I wonder how many golfers will read that, ignore it, and jump straight to the club speed section to hit it further ha ha ha ha…

Loads. :-)

I hope you enjoy this unique coaching manual and find it helpful.

Set Up

The focus of this coaching manual is the golf swing.

Set up, however, should never be overlooked. In fact, **it should be the first thing that is looked at -** When wanting to make improvements.

Here's why:

Let's say a right-handed golfer goes for a lesson because they are hitting the ball right of target. The strike is good. This golfer has an *open club face*.

Before changing anything in swing, you should look at all the influences of an open club face at set up…

This golfer could have a weak grip…

Problem solved.

(Sorry, this is golf)

"Problem… Less frequent."

Here is something I strongly believe:

"You can optimise your set up, to suit you. (Within reason)."

QUESTION:

Are you that golfer in the example with an open club face??? Do you think it's important to have a nice grip???

Before you answer yes and yes. Ask yourself this:

What is more important:

(i) Having a neutral grip at set up & missing the target right regularly.

Or

(ii) Having a strong grip at set up & hitting the target regularly?

Should you optimise your set Up???

Reading the conclusions on pages 178 - 181 might help you make a choice if undecided.

THE GRIP:

➢ Base of fingers - lead hand:

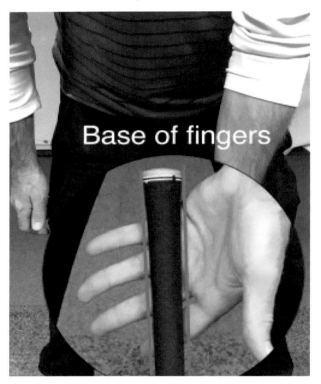

➢ V of lead hand pointing at sternum:

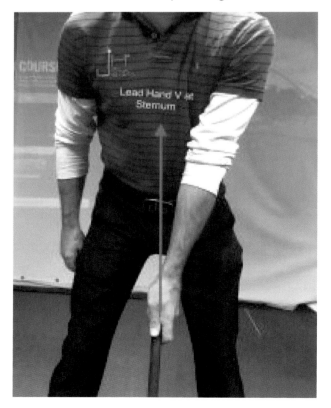

➢ 3 pinkie options:

i) Interlock

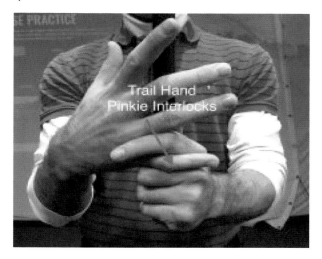

ii) Overlap:

iii) Baseball (10 finger grip):

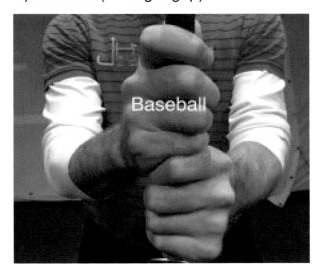

➢ Fleshy part of trail hand, sits on top of lead thumb:

➢ V of trail hand points to trail shoulder:

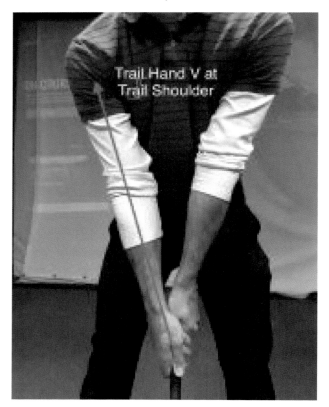

BALL POSITION:

➢ Centre for irons:

➢ Lead heel for Driver:

*NOTE: The ball position can be "optimised" to suit a player's tendencies:

When playing the ball position **<u>forwards</u> in the stance:**

(i) *The club face is more closed*

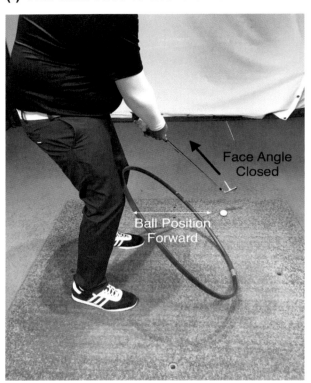

(ii) *The club path more inwards*

(iii) *The attack angle is shallower.*

Because impact is later in the arc.

When playing the ball position **backwards** in the stance:

(i) *The club face is more open*

(ii) *The club path more outwards*

(iii) *The attack angle is steeper.*

Because impact is earlier in the arc.

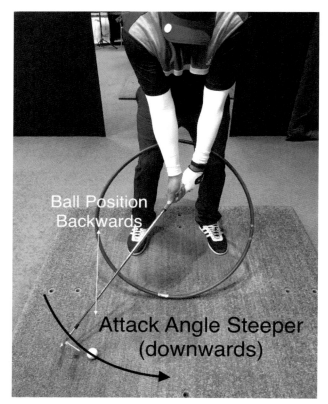

This is known as the 'D Plane & can be used to a golfer's advantage.

STANCE:

> Shoulder width for most irons. Can be narrower for shorter clubs and should be wider for the driver:

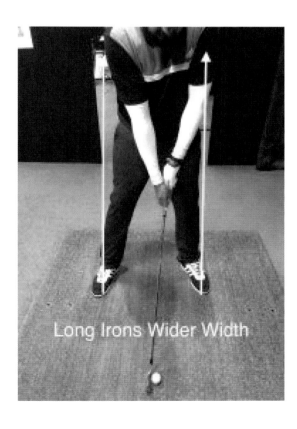

➢ Lead foot flayed. Allows pelvis to rotate more freely through impact:

➢ Lead hand level with lead peck creates a bit of forward shaft lean with the irons:

ALIGNMENT:

➤ Feet, knees, hips, torso, and shoulders. All parallel to target.

POSTURE:

Process:

> (i) Stand up straight.

(ii) Fingers down to kneecaps

(iii) Soften knees.

(iv) Pressure on the balls or arches of feet.

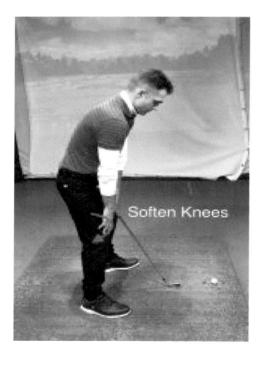

➤ v) Arms Hang under chin.

Take grip. Checking that trail hand has enough room to pass club and pelvis.

➢ Spine Angle wants to be "neutral."

Common pit falls:

C Shape Posture & *S Shape Posture*

Driver:

➤ Run fingers of trail hand down to trail knee.

This creates a slight shoulder angle tilt – ideal for the driver, with the ball on a tee.

Ranges of Movement – Ball, Club & Body

This chapter is the largest – because it is the foundation of the research. And yet… You don't even need to read it!

The reason for this chapter is to give you a greater understanding of how the research was developed.

This section has researched the **ball position**, the **club** and **10 major body parts**, (*upper & lower body*) assessing each of their Ranges of Movement [ROM].

You will see lots of technical / medical terms in this chapter. Such as flexion, extension, posterior, anterior, circumduction etc.

YOU DO NOT NEED TO KNOW OR REMEMBER THESE TERMS… In the Faults & Fixes sections: simplified, user friendly terms are used.

Some people may find these terms interesting / educational, that's why they have been recorded in this chapter.

*Knowing what these terms mean and more importantly – WHAT THEY DO. Has really helped me develop my research.

Allowing me to look at the golf swing "objectively" – fact based and measurable.

I have broken down what effects the golf shot, into 12 tangible components:

OUTSIDE AGENICES:

    (i)   The Ball

    (ii)   The Club

UPPER BODY

    (iii)   Hands

    (iv)   Wrists

    (v)   Elbows

    (vi)   Shoulders

    (vii)   Neck

    (viii)   Spine

LOWER BODY

    (ix)   Pelvis

    (x)   Knee

    (xi)   Ankle

    (xii)   Feet

In a nut shell: The ball, the club and 10 major joints in our skeletal system.

Each of these 12 components have Ranges of Movement [ROM].

Those ROM are outlined in the remainder of this chapter.

Every single ROM has been applied to every single SHOT TYPE.

Considering its effect at **Set Up**, **Impact** and in some chapters, Transition.

The most *dominant influences*, have been recorded in the Faults & Fixes.

OUTSIDE COMPONENTS:

Ball:

Forwards   &   Backwards.

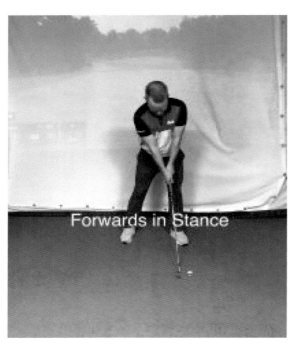 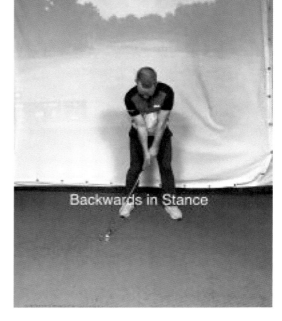

In front   &   Behind

Club:

Leaning forwards   &   Leaning backwards

Tilted Upwards   &   Tilted downwards.

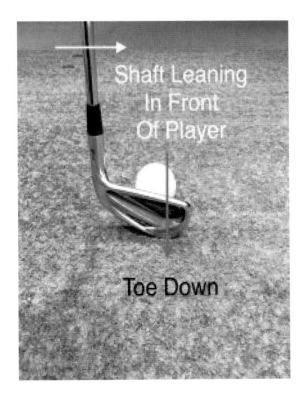 

Twisted open   &   Twisted closed.

(*Right* for a Right-Hander Player)   (*Left* for a Right-Handed Player)

NOTE:

The vertical (higher & lower) movement of the golf club can be seen immediately on the next page - with regard to the hands moving up and down.

Hands:

| Up (higher) | & | Down (lower) |

| Forwards | & | Backwards |

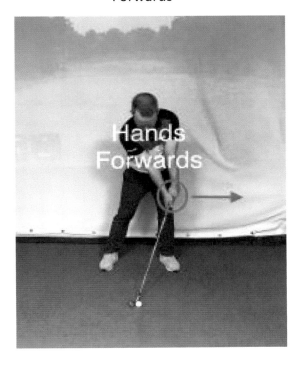

In front	&	Behind

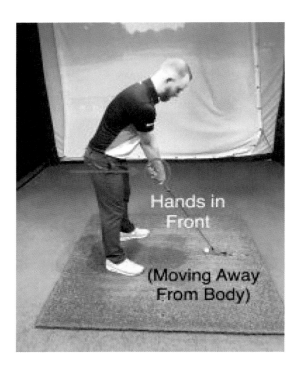 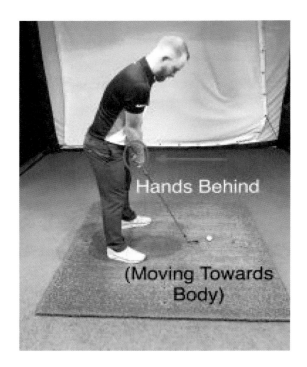

Strong grip	&	Weak grip

Placement High on Handle   &   Placement Low on Handle

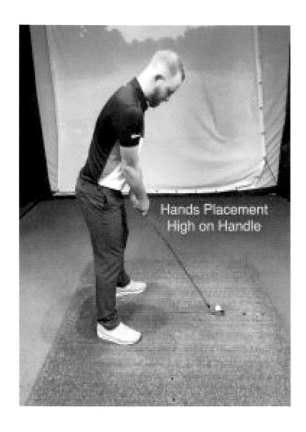

Grip Pressure (too soft / too firm)   or   Grip pressure good

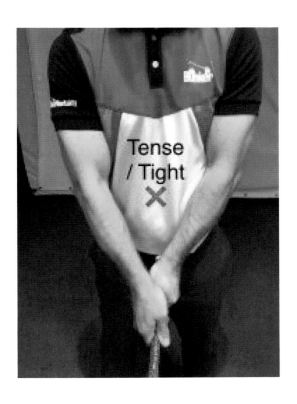
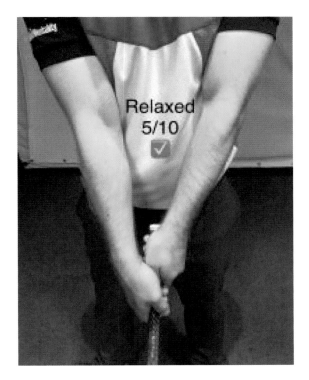

Wrists:

Flexion & Extension

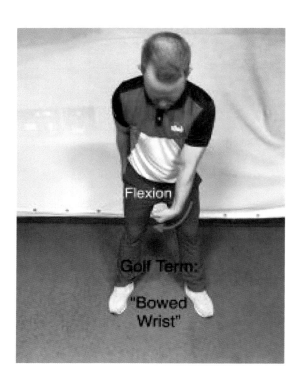 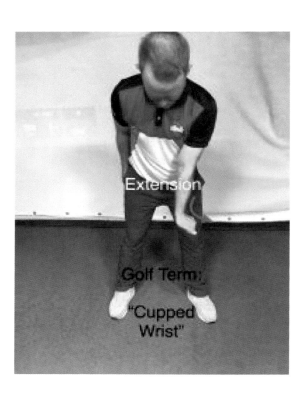

Supination & Pronation

Elbows:

Extension

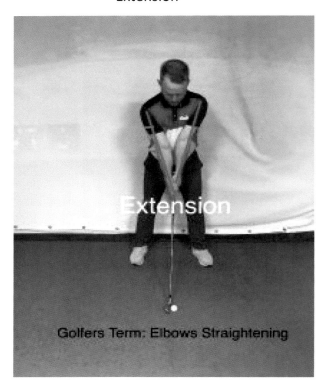

Flexion

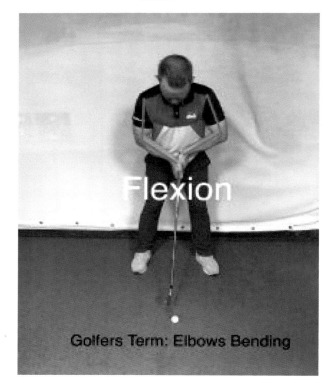

Shoulders:

Up (higher) & Down (lower)

 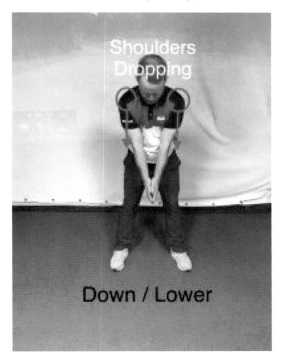

Abduction & Adduction

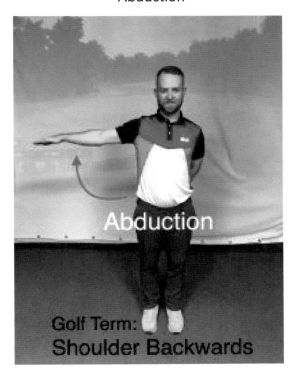 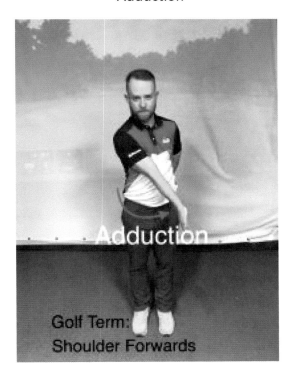

Flexion	&	Extension

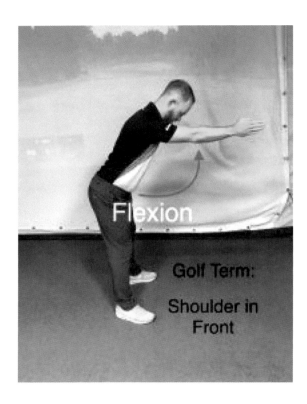 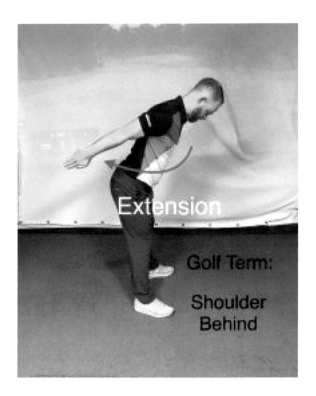

Internal rotation	&	External rotation

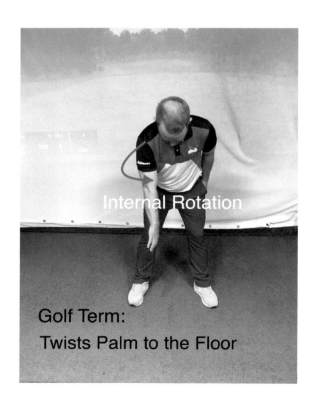 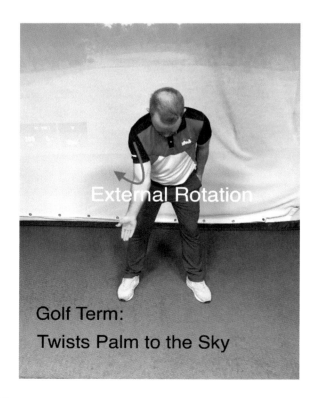

Neck:

Flexion & Extension

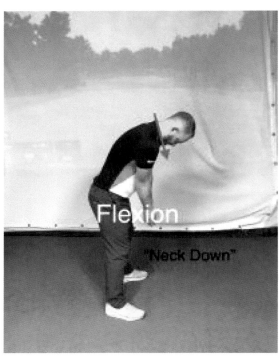 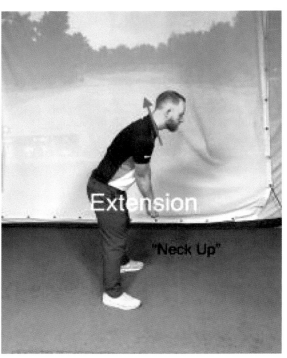

Tilted trail & Tilted lead

Twisted trail   &   Twisted lead.

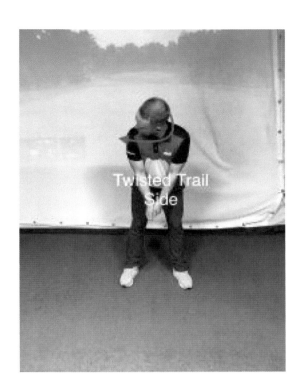 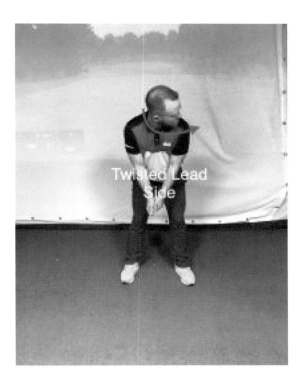

<u>Spine</u>:

Flexion   &   Extension

Trail side bend   &   Lead side bend

44

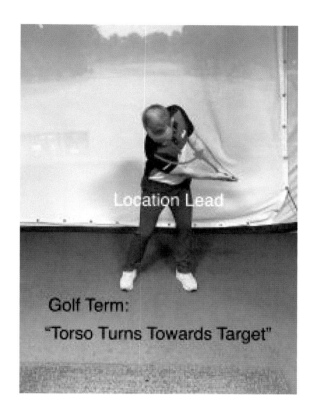

PHYSICAL COMPONENTS:

Lower Body:

Pelvis:

<table>
<tr><td>Posterior</td><td>&</td><td>Anterior</td></tr>
</table>

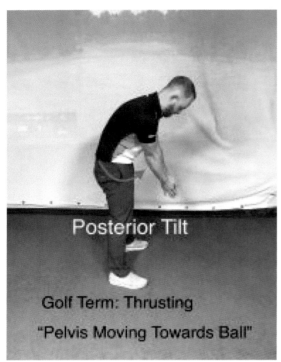

<table>
<tr><td>Location trail</td><td>&</td><td>Location lead</td></tr>
</table>

Elevation & Depression.

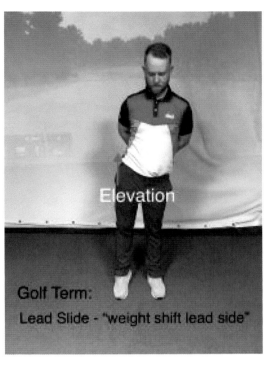

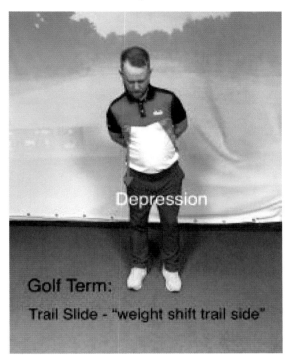

*Note

The pelvis can perform:

Abduction & Adduction

As well as:

Extension   &   Flexion

But these have not been considered for the effects on the golf shot, as the feet are lifted off the floor to perform these movements.

Knees:

Flexion

Extension

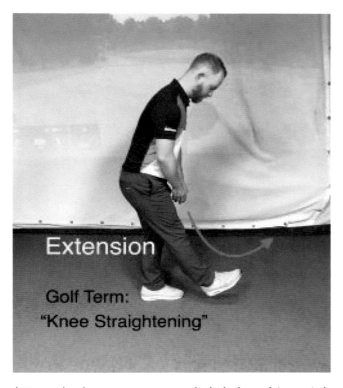

*Note the knee can rotate slightly but this mainly comes from the movement of the ankle.

Ankle, Feet & Toes:

Plantarflexion & Dorsiflexion

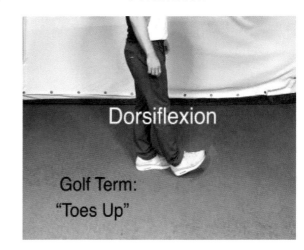

Abduction & Adduction

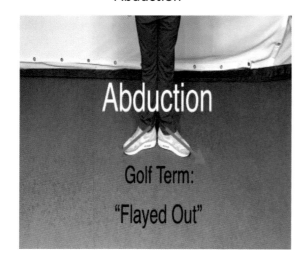

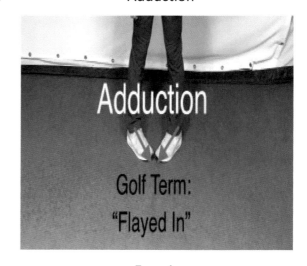

Inversion & Eversion

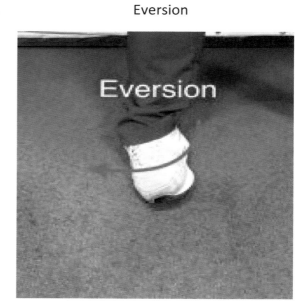

Wide & Narrow

 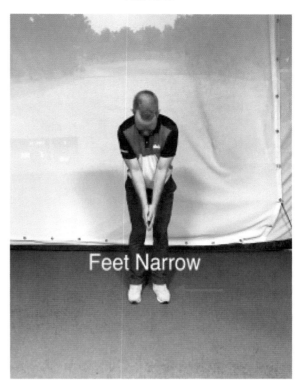

Weight lead side & Weight trail side

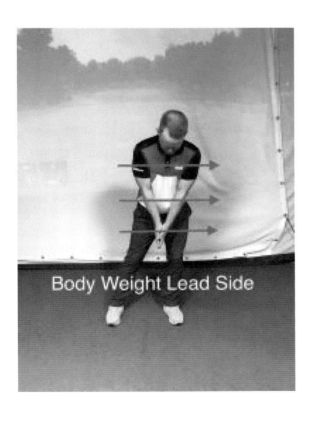 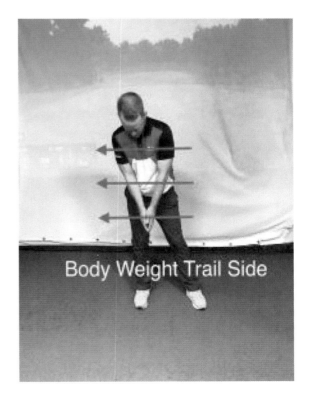

That concludes all the Ranges of Movements considered when writing the Faults and Fixes chapters. For each of the 11 SHOT TYPES.

Thin Shots:

What is it?

Club striking the ball on the bottom of the club head.

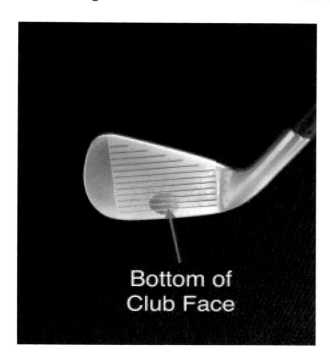

Extreme thin shots are when the leading edge strikes the ball.

*Note.

A topped shot is when the sole of the club strikes the ball. This is the result of either an extreme thin shot, or an extremely steep angle of attack (think chopping wood with an axe). If you're topping the ball, you need to clarify WHY, before heading to the relevant section of 'Faults & Fixes.'

If you hardly take a divot, you are *likely* in the "**extreme thin category**."

If you take big divots with your irons, you are *likely* in the "**steep angle of attack category**."

Thin Shots:

Set Up - Faults and Fixes:

Dominant Influences:

(1.) Ball- position forward in the stance. Club travelling more "on the up" at impact.

(2.) Knees- too straight. Club higher.

(3.) Spine- too upright. **Hands higher.**

(4.) Feet- too narrow. **Hands & Club higher.**

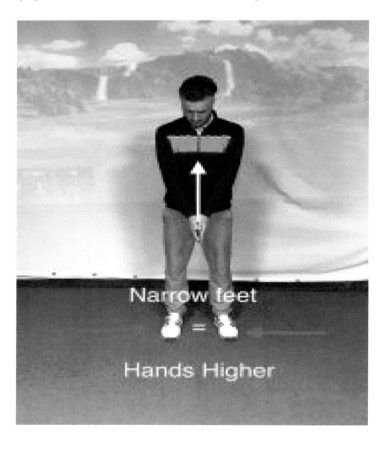

(5.) Feet- pressure in heels. Hands move up when in golf posture.

Thin Shots:

Impact - Faults and Fixes:

Dominant Influences:

(1) Hands- lifting up. Lifts club up.

(2) Shoulders- up. Club up.

(3) Elbows- bending. **Club up.**

(4) Knees- straightening. **Club up.**

(5) Spine / Neck- lifting up. **Club up.**

(6) Pelvis- thrusting towards golf ball. **Hands move up / club up.**

(7) Lead wrist- cupping. **Club moves forwards and up.**

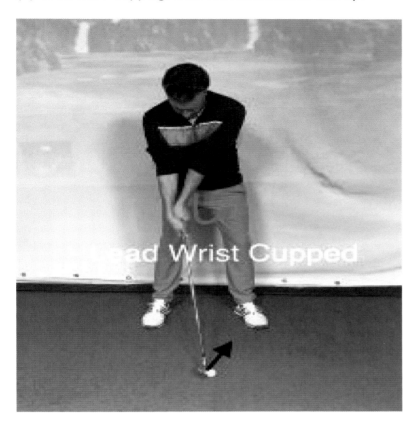

(8) Wrists- radial (thumbs up). **Club up.**

Fat Shots:

What is it?

When the club head strikes the ground before the ball.

With an iron, ball then turf contact is preferred. It is only a fat shot if hitting the ground first.

Before the Ball

After the Ball ✓

Fat Shots:

Set Up - Faults and Fixes:

Dominant Influences:

(1) Feet- Weight on back foot. Encourages club to hit ground first.

(2) Spine- Dropping downwards. Club lower.

(3) Knees- too bent. **Hands lower.**

(4) Feet- too wide apart. **Drops hands lower.**

(5) Feet- Pressure in toes. **Hands move down when in golf posture.**

Fat Shots:

Impact - Faults and Fixes:

Dominant Influences:

(1) Hands- lower. **Club lower.**

(2) Shoulders- down. **Club down.**

(3) Elbows- straightening. **Club downwards.**

(4) Feet- weight trail side. **Encourages club to hit ground first.**

(5) Spine- dropping downwards. **Club moves downwards.**

(6) Hands- Backwards, staying behind the ball. **Encourages club to hit ground first.**

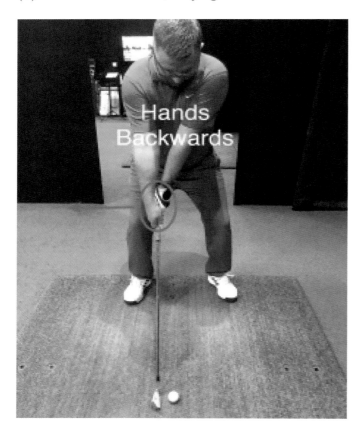

(7) Wrists ulna. Thumbs down. **Club down.**

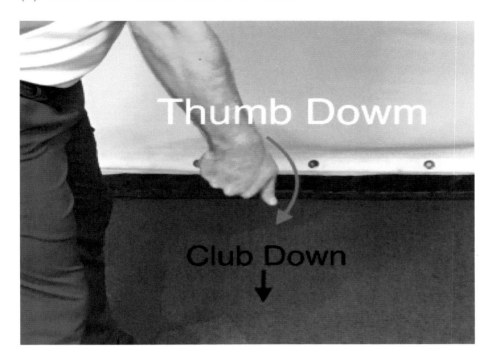

(8) Knees- bending. **Club down.**

(9) Spine: Trail side bend. **Encourages club to hit ground first.**

(10) Feet- Pressure moving into toes. **Club will move down when in golf posture.**

Toe Strike:

What is it?

When the ball is struck, out the toe end of the club.

*A right-handed golfer can be launching the ball right of target, assuming they have an *open club face*. However, it might be worth checking the strike. Because an extreme toe strike will open the club face.

A closed club face can cause a toe strike, as it presents the toe of the club, to the ball.

Toe Strike:

Set Up - Faults and Fixes:

Dominant Influences:

(1) Hands- too close to body. Pulls club, closer to body.

(2) Ball- In front / standing too far away. Promotes a toe strike at impact.

(3) Feet- Pressure in heels. **Moves club, closer to body.**

(4) Ball- Position forward in stance. **Promotes a toe strike, around the swing arc.**

(5) Feet- weight trail side. Promotes a toe strike, around the swing arc – see **influence 4** on **page 74.**

75

Toe Strike:

Impact - Faults and Fixes:

Dominant Influences:

(1) Hands- moving closer to body. **Pulls club closer to body.**

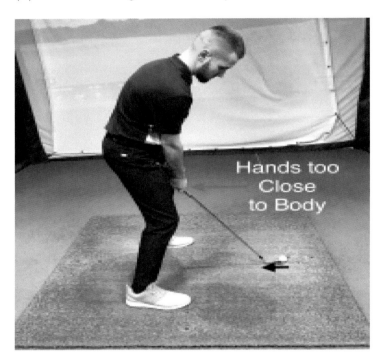

(2) Elbows- bending. Moves club inwards. **Pulls club closer to body.**

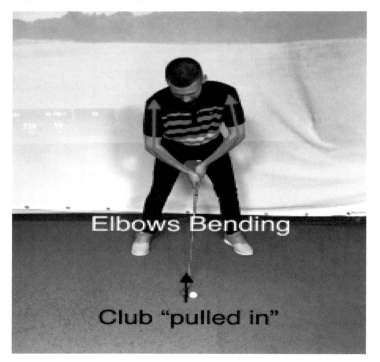

(3) Club & Hands- Staying backwards. Presenting toe of the club to the ball & club path more inwards.

See image on **page 72** & **Influence 4** on **page 74.**

(4) Shoulders- Up. **Moves club in closer to body.**

(5) Shoulder- Behind. **Pulls club in towards body.**

(6) Trail shoulder, staying backwards. Presenting the toe to the ball & club path inwards.

See image on page 72 & Influence 4 on page 74.

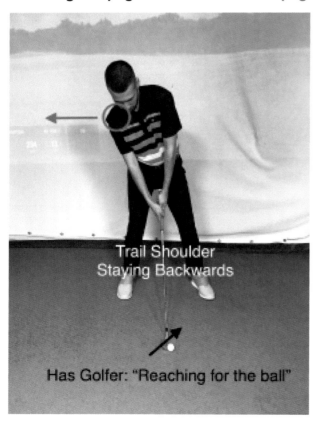

(7) Feet- moving pressure into heels. **Club moves in closer to body.**

(8) Wrist- Ulna. Thumbs down. **Club works down and in towards body.**

(9) Spine- Lifting up. **Pulls hands in closer to body.**

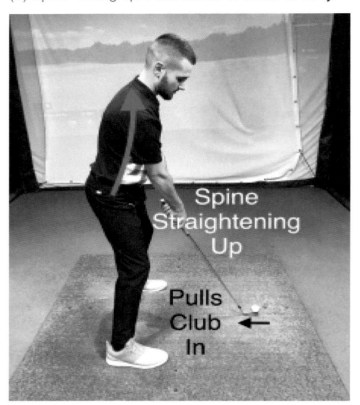

(10) Feet- Weight on back foot. Swing arc works "more inwards". **See image** on **page 72** & **Influence 4** on **page 74.**

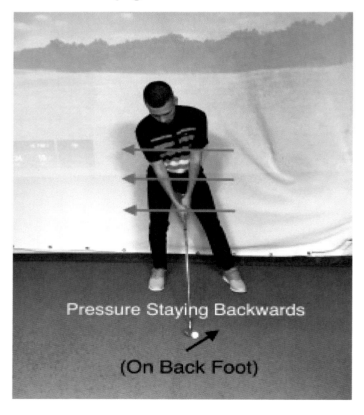

(11) Wrist- Lead wrist bowed. **Moves club in closer to body.**

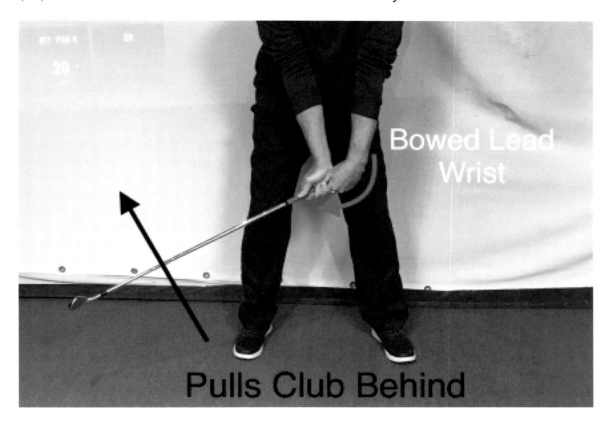

(12) Ankle- Toes up, puts pressure into heels. **Moves club in closer to body.**

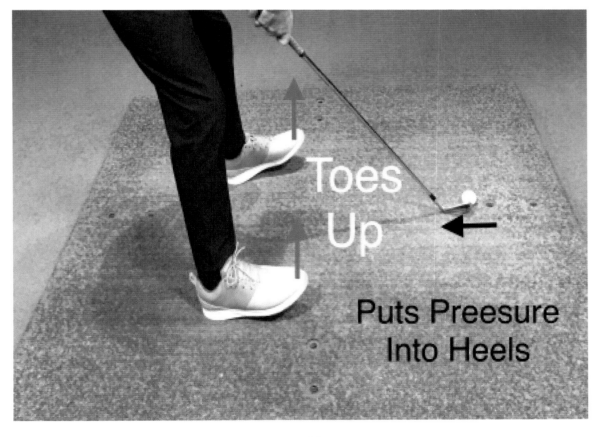

Heel Strike:

What is it?

When the ball is struck, out the heel of the club.

An extreme heel strike with an iron will cause a shank. A shank happens when the club, strikes the ball, between the place where the club face, meets the club shaft. More commonly known as the hosel.

An open club face can cause a heel strike, as it presents the heel of the club, to the ball.

Heel Strike:

Set Up - Faults and Fixes:

Dominant Influences:

(1) Ball- Behind / Standing too close. Promotes a heel strike at impact.

(2) Hands- Too far away from body. Pushes heel of club, away from body.

(3) Feet- Pressure in toes. **Pushes heel of club, away from body.**

(4) Ball- position back in stance. **Promotes a heel strike, around the swing arc.**

(5) Feet- Weight lead side. Promotes a heel strike, because of the swing arc – **see influence 4 at the bottom of page 85.**

Heel Strike:

Impact - Faults and Fixes:

Dominant Influences:

(1) Hands- Moving away from body. **Club moves away from body.**

(2) Shoulders- down or in front. **Pushes club away from body.**

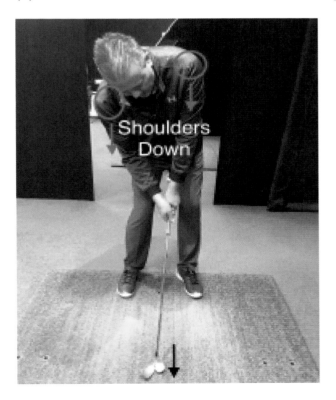

(3) Elbows- straightening. **Pushes club away from body.**

(4) Feet- Pressure moving into toes. **Moves club in a direction away from the body.**

(5) Wrist- Lead cupping. **Pushes club in front of body.**

(6) Hands- Forwards & club shaft forwards. Opens club face, presenting heel to the ball. See image on **page 83** & **Influence 4** on **page 85.**

(7) Shoulder- trail shoulder, moving ahead of ball. Opens club face, presenting heel to ball.

See image on **page 83** & **Influence 4** on **page 85.**

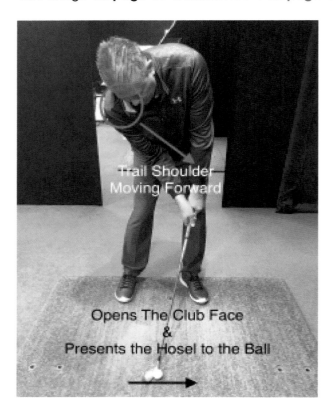

(8) Feet- weight lead side. Club path travels more "outwards in the swing arc.

See **influence 4** at Set Up on **page 85.**

(9) Knee- Bending. **Pushes club in front of body.**

(10) Spine and neck- Moving downwards. **Pushes club in front of body.**

(11) Wrist- Radial. Thumbs up. **Moves club up and in front of body.**

Open Club Face:

What is it?

An open face is when, for a RH handed golfer, the club face points right of target.

This section assumes centre strike and assumes the golfer is aiming parallel to the target.

Parallel to the target, meaning parallel to the ball to target line.

NOTE: An extreme toe strike will open the club face. Sometimes the golfer assumes they have an open face. But in fact, it's a strike issue. See toe strike and face opening below:

NOTE: An extreme heel strike with an iron, can cause the ball to go right (RH Golfer). This is a strike issue and not to be confused with an open face. See heel strike and ball flight below:

Open Club Face:

Set Up - Faults and Fixes:

Dominant Influences:

(1) Hands- Weak grip. Thumbs too far over towards target side, encourages an open face.

(2) Club- Aiming open. Club face itself pointing in an open direction, at address.

(3) Hands- forward & Club Shaft Forward. **Points the club face open.**

(4) Ball- backwards in stance (D Plane). Face angle more open in the swing arc. **See image bottom page 19.**

(5) Shoulder- Trail shoulder twisted open (Think: palm of trail hand turns towards the sky).

Twists forearms open and points club face open.

Open Club Face:

Impact - Faults and Fixes:

Dominant Influences:

(1) Wrists- Palm of lead hand, turns towards the floor. "Rolling the wrists open."

(2) Wrists- Cupped lead wrist. **Opens the club face.**

(3) Hands- Forward & Club shaft forward. **Pushes the club face open.**

(4) Shoulders- Trail shoulder moving forwards. **Leans club shaft forwards and opens the face**

(5) Shoulder- Trail shoulder, twisting open. Think: "palm of trail hand turns to the sky." **Rolls the club face open.**

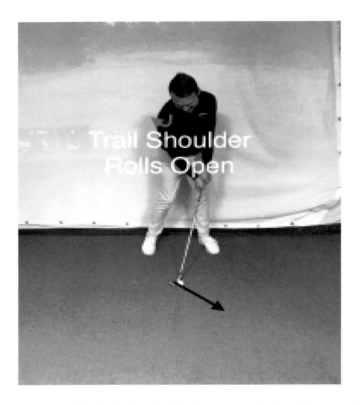

(6) Feet- Weight lead side. **Leans club shaft forwards and opens the club face.**

(7) Wrists- Ulna (thumbs down). **Tilts the toe of club downwards and opens the club face. See image bottom left of page 31** (tilted downwards). AKA: Face plane tilt.

Closed Club Face:

What is it?

A closed face is when for a RH handed golfer, the club face points left of target.

This section assumes centre strike and assumes the golfer is aiming parallel to the target.

Parallel to target, meaning parallel to the ball to target line.

An extreme heel strike can cause the ball to go left for a RH handed golfer, this is a ball striking issue and not to be confused with a closed club face.

*Note - not considering the gear effect on some drivers

Closed Club Face:

Set Up - Faults and Fixes:

Dominant Influences:

(1) Hands- Strong grip. Thumbs too far over, away from target, encourages a closed face.

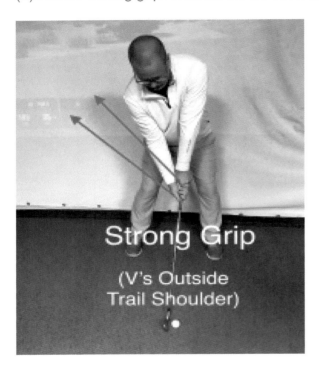

(2) Club- aiming closed. Club face itself pointing in a closed direction, at address.

(3) Hands backwards & Shaft backwards. **Leans club backwards and closes the face.**

(4) Ball- forwards in stance (D plane). **Face angle more closed in the swing arc. See image top of page 18** in Set Up.

(5) Shoulder- Trail shoulder twisted closed. (Think: palm of trail hand turns towards the floor) Twists forearms closed and points club face closed.

(6) Hands- Low. Tilts toe of club up & closes face plane tilt. *Is more influential at impact.

Closed Club Face:

Impact - Faults and Fixes:

Dominant Influences:

(1) Wrists- Palm of trail hand, turns towards the floor. "Turning the toe over."

(2) Wrists- Bowed lead wrist. Closes the club face.

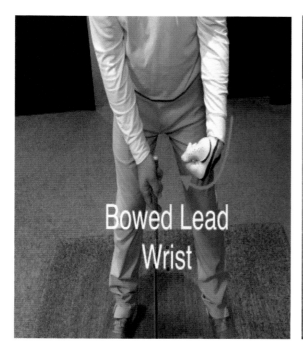

(3) Hands- Staying back behind the ball. **Leans club back and closes the face.**

(4) Shoulders- Trail shoulder, twisting closed. Think: "palm of trail hand turns to the floor."
Rolls the club face closed.

(5) Shoulders- trail shoulder staying back behind the ball. **Leans the shaft back and closes the club face.**

(6) Feet- Weight trail side. **Leans club shaft back and closes the club face.**

(7) Hands- Moving too low. **Will tilt toe upwards and close the club face.** *Could also cause the heel of the club to "dig in" to the ground and dramatically turn the club face over.

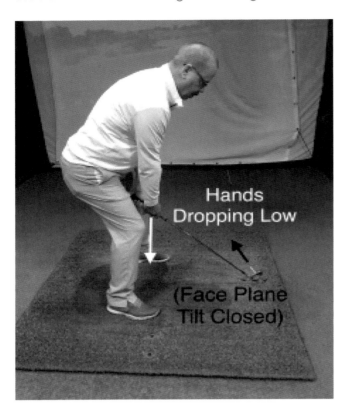

(8) Wrists- Radial (thumbs up) **Tilts toe of club upwards and closes the club face. See image bottom right page 31** (tilted upwards). AKA: Face plane tilt.

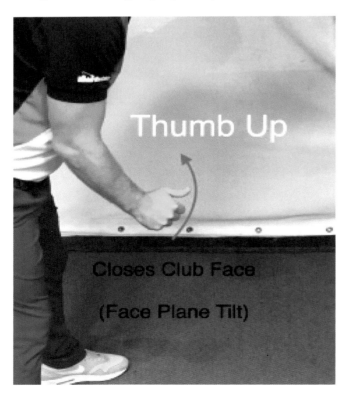

Club Path - Out to In:

What is it?

The direction the club head travels through impact. Assuming a centre strike has been made, the club path largely influences the curve on the ball.

An Inward club path is termed "**Out to In**." SEE BLUE LINE BELOW:

When a golfer's club path is "Out to In:" the most destructive shot in their game is *usually* a slice. (RH golfer - ball curves right of target).

Their good shots are a fade.

(RH golfer ball starts left of target and finishes on target).

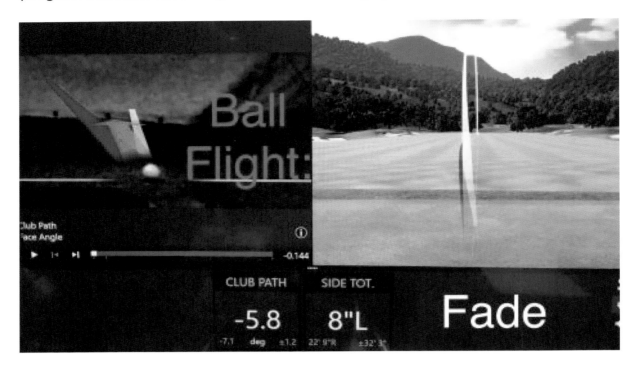

If a golfer purposely wants to fade the ball, they must have an Out to In club path.

Club Path - Out to In:

Set Up - Faults and Fixes:

Dominant Influences:

(1) SHOULDERS, TORSO, PELVIS, KNEES & FEET: ALIGNMENT- Parallel to target. If any of these are "open," they will influence a more "out to in" club path.

(2) Hands- Weak grip. Twists forearm alignment open.

(3) Ball- Forwards in stance (D plane). **Club then works more "inwards," in the swing arc.**

See image bottom page 18 in Set Up.

(4) Feet- Weight trail side. **Swing arc works inwards, sooner.**

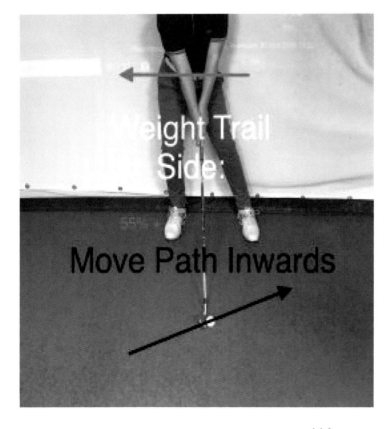

(5) Feet- pressure in heels. **Works the club, more inwards.**

(6) Neck- Chin down. **Limits shoulder turn, limiting hand depth.** See influence (7) in transition. **Page 119.**

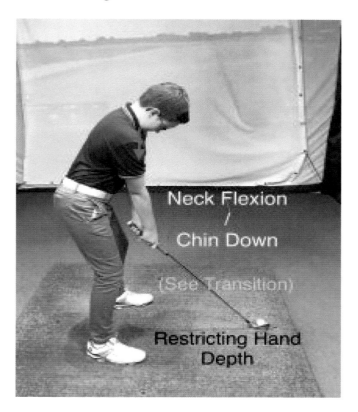

Club Path - Out to In:

Top of Backswing - Faults and Fixes:

Dominant Influences:

(1) Elbows- Extending (casting). **Moves club out in front of golfer.**

(2) Hands- Moving in front of the body. **Moves club, out in front of golfer.**

(3) Shoulders- Trail shoulder twists in. Think: "palm of trail hand turns towards the ground."
This moves the club out in front of the golfer.

(4) Spine- Torso turning too quickly to target – "Spinning out of it." Club moves out in front.

(5) Pelvis- Pelvis turning too quickly to the target. **Club moves out in front.**

(6) Feet- Weight staying trail side. **Club works "inwards," sooner, in the swing arc.**

(7) Neck- **Chin down limits shoulder turn, limiting potential hand depth. (The club can't get as far "behind" the golfer)** See influence (6) at Set Up. **Page 115.**

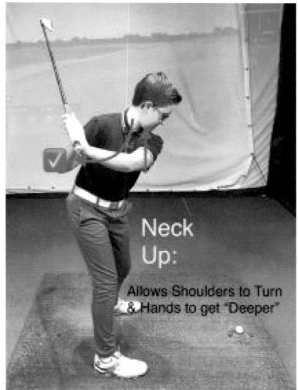

(8) Shoulders- Staying high. **If body turns from here, hands will move and stay out in front.**

(9) Wrists- Lead wrist cupped. **Club works in front of the golfer.**

(10) Knee- Bending trail knee. **Opens up body alignment.**

(11) Spine- Lead side bend. **Opens body alignment and moves club path inwards.**

Club Path - Out to In:

Impact - Faults and Fixes:

Dominant Influences:

(1) Elbows- Bending. Pulls club in closer to golfer, moving club path inwards.

(2) Shoulders- Up and Behind. Pulls club in closer to golfer and moves club path inwards.

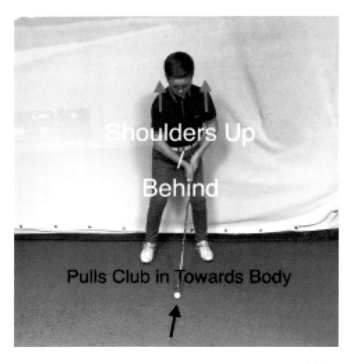

(3) Feet- Weight staying on trail side. **Club works "inwards," sooner, in the swing arc.**

(4) Feet- Pressure moving into heels. **Moves club in closer to body and moves club path** inwards.

(5) Hands & Club- Staying behind ball. **Club works inwards sooner, in the swing arc.**

(6) Shoulders- Trail shoulder staying behind ball. **Club works inwards, sooner, in the swing arc.**

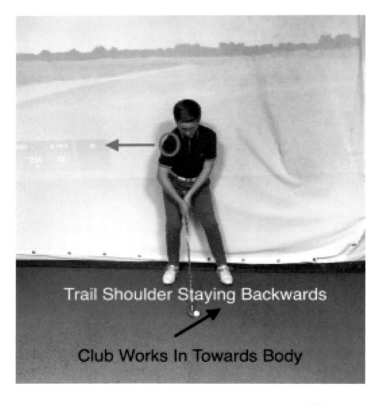

(7) Ankle- Toes coming up in the air. Moving club in closer to body and moving club path inwards.

Club Path - In to Out:

What is it?

The direction the club head travels through impact. Assuming a centre strike has been made, the club path largely influences the curve on the ball.

An outward club path is termed "**In to Out**." SEE BLUE LINE BELOW:

When a golfer's club path is "In to Out:" the most destructive shot in their game is *usually* a hook. (RH golfer – ball curves left of target).

Their good shots are a draw. (RH golfers ball starts right of target and finishes on target).

If a golfer purposely wants to draw the ball, they must have an In to Out club path.

Club Path - In to Out:

Set Up - Faults and Fixes:

Dominant Influences:

(1) SHOULDERS, TORSO, PELVIS, KNEES & FEET: ALIGNMENT- Parallel to target. If any of these are closed, they will influence a more "in to out" club path.

(2) Hands- Strong grip. V's outside trail shoulder. Twists forearm alignment closed.

(3) Ball- Position back in the stance, (D Plane). Club then works more "outwards," in the swing arc. **See image top of page 20 in** Set Up.

(4) Feet- Weight lead side. Club works more "outwards," in swing arc.

(5) Neck- Chin up. **Helps shoulder turn at top of backswing.** See influence (7) in transition.

Page 134.

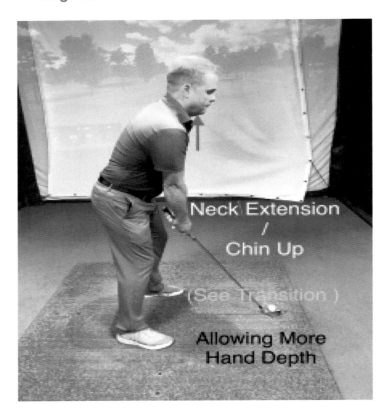

(6) Feet- pressure in toes. **Works club more "away" from golfer (outwards).**

Club Path - In to Out:

Transition - Faults and Fixes:

Dominant Influences:

(1) Hands- Move "behind" body. Club more in to out, from this position.

(2) Shoulders- Trail shoulder twists out. Think: "palm of trail hand turns towards the sky."
This moves the club behind the golfer.

(3) Spine- Location stays pointing trail. **Keeping hand depth. Keeping club "behind" the golfer.**

(4) Wrists- Bowing the lead wrist. **Works the club behind the golfer.**

(5) Elbows- Trail elbow bends. **Working the club "behind" the golfer. Think: "the opposite of casting.**

(6) Pelvis- Location stays pointing trail. **Think: pelvis stays pointing away from target.**

(7) Neck- From influence (5) at Set Up. **Page 130.** Chin up increases potential shoulder turn, increasing hand depth.

(8) Shoulders- Trail shoulder moves forward & down. **Shaft "flattens"** <u>behind</u> the golfer.

(9) Shoulders- Trail shoulder moving down, before turning. **Keeps the club "behind" the golfer.**

(10) Wrists- Radial, thumb up. **Works the club behind the golfer.**

(11) Knee- Bending lead knee. **Closes body alignment. Moving club path, more "in to out."**

(12) Feet- Weight moving lead side. **Club path works more "outwards," in the swing arc.**

(13) Pelvis- Thrusting towards ball. **Club works more "behind" the golfer.**

(14) Spine- Trail side bend. **Moves the club more "behind the golfer."**

Club Path - In to Out:

Impact - Faults and Fixes:

Dominant Influences:

(1) Elbows- Trail straightening. **Pushes club away from golfer, moving club path outwards.**

(2) Hands & Club- Moving ahead of ball. **Club works path more "outwards," in the swing arc.**

(3) Wrists- Bowed lead wrist. Works the club more, "behind" the golfer.

(4) Shoulders- Down. Pushes club in front of golfer, and moves club path outwards.

(5) Feet- Weight moving to lead side. **Club works more outwards, in the swing arc.**

(6) Shoulders- Trail shoulder moving forwards. **Club works more "outwards" in the swing arc.**

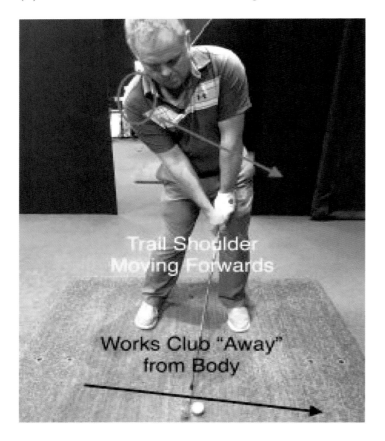

(7) Feet- Pressure moving into toes. Moves club away from body and moves club path outwards.

Attack Angle Shallower:

What is it?

The club moving more "upwards" through impact.

Why would you want to make the attack angler shallower?

If you can make the attack angle "shallower" (more on the up) with the driver. You can increase your maximum distance.

This is true, but if you are already inaccurate with your driver, the likelihood is, this will make you even more inaccurate.

Some golfers, with slower swing speeds can benefit from a shallower attack angle (AKA more "on the" up) to achieve greater distance.

See image below:

Golfer on the left	Golfer on the right
Swinging at **100mph.**	Swinging at **93mph** – *7mph slower*
Their attack angle is **-2.4** (*down*).	Their attack angle is **+2.8** (*up*).
Giving them a spin rate **3430rpm.**	Giving them a spin rate of **2160rpm.**
& a carry distance of **218 yards.**	& a carry distance of **233 yards**

Although the golfer on the right is 7mph slower. Their attack angle is helping them achieve a better spin rate, which is helping them achieve a greater distance.

15 YARDS FURTHER. Despite being 7MPH SLOWER.

Attack Angle Shallower:

Set Up - Faults and Fixes:

Dominant Influences:

(1) Ball- Position forward in the stance. **Encourages more "hitting on the up."**

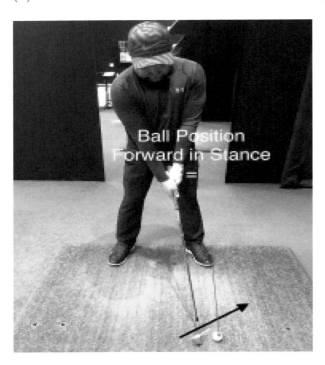

(2) Feet- Weight on the back foot. **Encourages more of an "upward" hit, at impact.**

(3) Shoulders- Trail shoulder lower. **This tilt, encourages more of an "upward" hit, at impact.**

(4) Spine- Upright. **Moving club more upwards. *Is more influential at impact**

(5) Feet- A narrow stance = Higher hands. **Higher hands = a shallower club head at impact.**

(6) Spine- Trail side bend. **Produces tilt in shoulder angle. This tilt, encourages more of an "upward" hit, at impact.**

(7) Hands- Grip in palms (less hinge). **See text below image:**

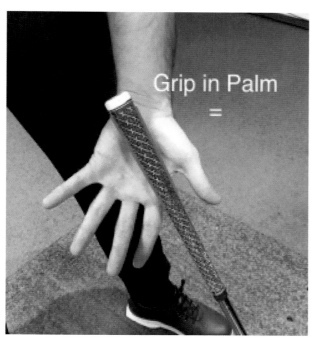

*NOTE- THIS IS MORE OF A FAULT THAN A FIX!!!

Do not do this in an attempt to be shallower.

(8) Hands- Backwards, behind ball. Leans the shaft backwards. Encouraging more of an "upward" hit, at impact. ***Is more influential at impact**

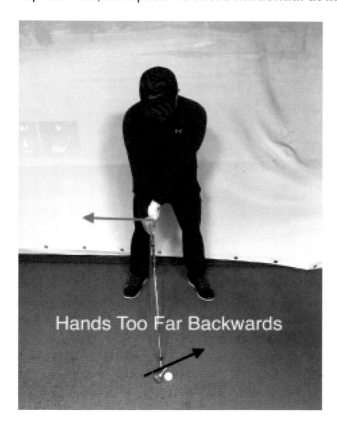

(9) Neck- Tilted towards trail side. Creates a tilt in shoulder angles. This tilt, encourages more of an "upward" hit, at impact.

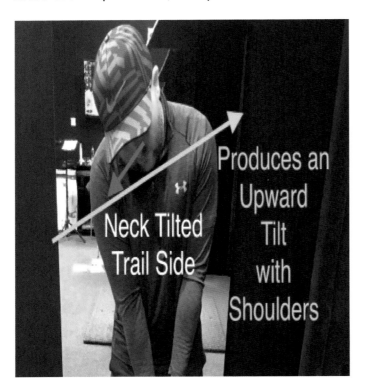

(10) Ball- In front. (Standing far away) Encourages golfer to swing "flatter & shallower."

(11) Ankle- Lead ankle flayed in. Makes it difficult for a golfer to transfer their weight. With less weight on the lead side, this influences more of an "upward" hit.

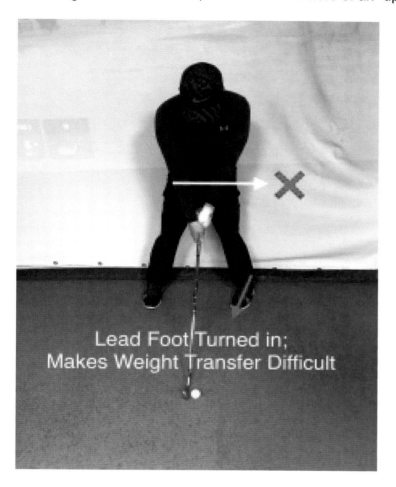

NOTE: THIS IS MORE OF A FAULT THAN A FIX!

Do not to this in attempt to be "shallower."

Attack Angle Shallower:

Impact - Faults and Fixes:

Dominant Influences:

(1) Hands- Moving Up. Moving the club away from the ground.

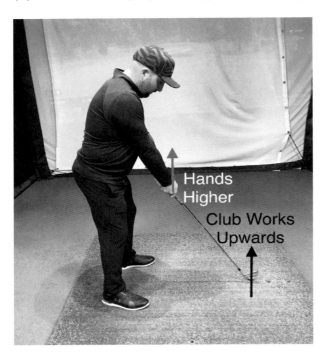

(2) Elbows- Bending. Pulling the club away from the ground.

(3) Shoulders- Trail shoulder staying behind ball. **Club then moves more "upwards:"**

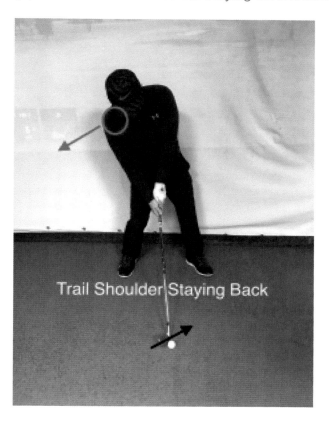

Trail Shoulder Staying Back

(4) Wrists- Cupping the lead wrist. **Moves club forwards in the arc. Becoming "shallower."**

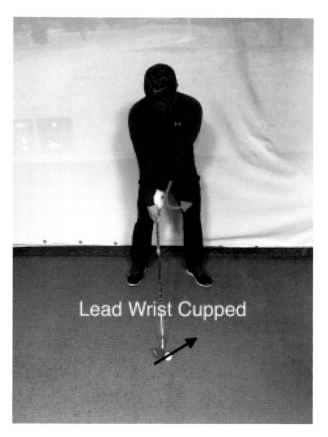

Lead Wrist Cupped

(5) Shoulders- Moving Up. **Moves the club away from the ground.**

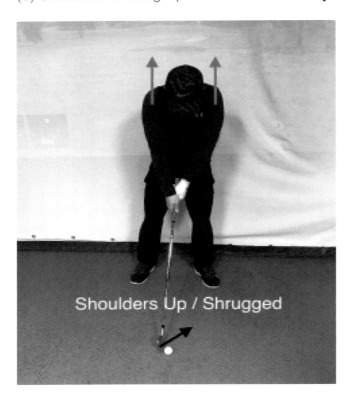

(6) Spine- Lifting Up. **Moves the club away from the ground.**

(7) Hands- Backwards, behind ball. Leans the shaft backwards. **Encouraging more of an "upward" hit.**

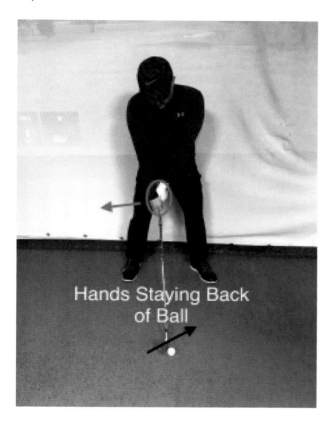

(8) Feet- Weight on the back foot. **Encourages more of an "upward" hit.**

(9) Pelvis- Moving towards the ball. **Moves the club up and away from the ground.**

(10) Knees- Straightening. **Moves the club away from the ground.**

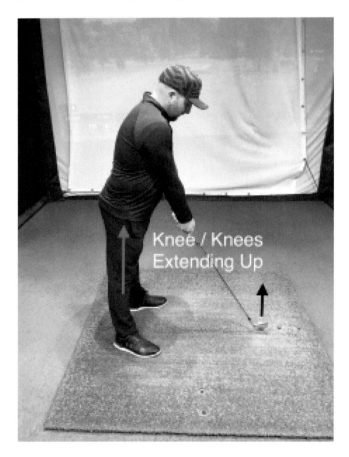

(11) Feet- Pressure moving into heels. **Moves the club up and away from the ground.**

(12) Wrists- Radial (thumbs up). **Moves the club up and away from the ground.**

(13) Ankle- Toes coming up. Encourages pressure into the heels of the feet, influencing the club to move up and away from the ground.

Attack Angle Steeper:

What is it?

The club moving more "downwards" through impact.

Why would you want to make the attack angler steeper?

Normally desirable for the golfer who wants to take a divot and "hit down" more with their irons.

Attack Angle Steeper:

Set Up - Faults and Fixes:

Dominant Influences:

(1) Spine- Lead side bend. Produces tilt in shoulder angle. This tilt, encourages more of a "downward" hit, at impact.

(2) Weight – On the front foot. Encourages more of a "downward" hit, at impact.

(3) Ball- Position back in stance. **Encourages more of a "downward" hit, at impact.**

(4) Grip- Grip in fingers (allows for more wrist hinge) **Enabling the club to come in, "steeper."**

(5) Shoulders- Trail shoulder higher. **This tilt, encourages more of a "downward" hit, at impact.**

(6) Hands- Forwards, ahead of ball. Leans the shaft forwards. **Encouraging more of a "downward" hit, at impact. *Is more influential at impact.**

(7) Feet- A wider stance = Lower hands. **Lower** hands = a steeper club head at impact.

(8) Spine- Dropping downwards. **Moving club downwards. *Is more influential at impact**

(9) Ball- Behind. (Standing close) **Encourages a golfer to swing more "upright & steeper."**

(10) Ankle- Lead ankle flayed out. **Makes it easier for a golfer to transfer their weight. More weight on the lead side, influences a more "downward" hit.**

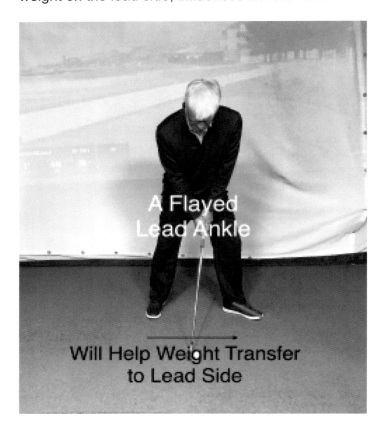

Attack Angle Steeper:

Impact - Faults and Fixes:

Dominant Influences:

(1) Hands- Moving Down. Moving the club down towards the ground.

(2) Elbows- Straightening. Pushing the club down towards the ground.

(3) Feet- Weight on the front foot. **Encourages more of a "downward" hit.**

(4) Shoulders- Moving Down. **Moves the club down towards the ground.**

(5) Hands- Forwards, in front of ball. Leans the shaft forwards. **Encouraging more of a "downward" hit.**

(6) Wrists- Bowing the lead wrist. **Moves the club backwards in the arc. Becoming "steeper."**

(7) Shoulder- Trail shoulder moving ahead of ball. **From here, club comes in "steeper."**

(8) Knees- Bending. **Moves the club down towards the ground.**

(9) Wrists- Ulna (thumbs down). **Moves the club down towards the ground.**

(10) Spine- Moving Down. **Moves the club down towards the ground.**

(11) Feet- Pressure moving in to the toes. **Moves the club lower towards the ground.**

(12) Pelvis- Moving away from the ball. **Moves the club down towards the ground.**

Increase Club Speed:

What is it?

Simply put:

How fast you swing the club.

Club speed is the single biggest factor in determining how far a player can "potentially" hit the ball.

Although speed is the biggest factor for maximum distance, efficiency plays a big role... Some golfers who swing at 100mph, hit the ball further than golfers who swing at 105mph.

How? Many factors. Strike being the most obvious.

Below is an image to highlight how a golfer who swings at 100mph, can hit the ball 30 yards further, than someone who swings at 105mph.

*Slower swing speed on the left but 30 yards further.

Not everyone should try to increase their club speed. (Especially with irons). So many golfers in their quest for more distance, lose accuracy and end shooting worse scores in the long run.

HOWEVER:

This is the 'Increase Club Speed' section and it has to said:

"Hitting the driver further is a HUGE advantage!!!"

BUT... You need to be able to swing faster, strike the centre of the club face AND... Still find fairways.

If you can do that (without breaking your back) – Then obviously, you should implement more speed into your golf.

A SIDE NOTE TO CONSIDER:

(i)   As this section is focused on hitting the ball further - it has to be said that having properly *custom fitted clubs* will help you maximise your distance.

(ii)   As will playing the right golf ball.

Increase Club Speed:

Set Up - Faults and Fixes:

Dominant Influences:

(1) Hands- Light grip pressure. **Allows club to "release" easier.**

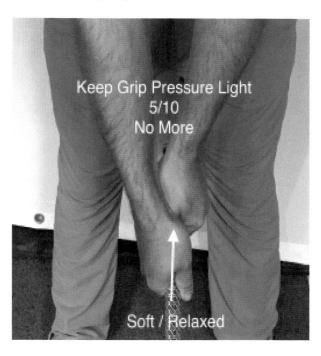

(2) Hands- Grip in fingers. **Allows for more wrist hinge, increasing potential club speed.**

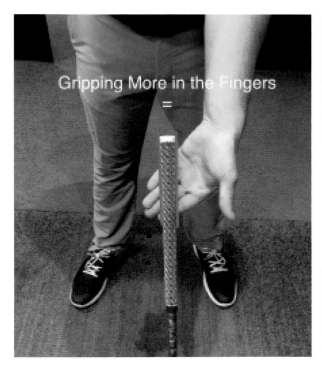

(3) Feet- Flayed out. **Allows golfer to turn more. Increasing turn can = increased club speed.**

(4) Feet- Pressure on balls of feet. **Makes weight transference easier.**

Increase Club Speed:

Transition - Faults and Fixes:

Dominant Influences:

(1) Shoulders & Hands- Higher. Higher hands = Longer swing, increasing speed.

(2) Spine & Pelvis- Turning away from target. A big shoulder turn can increase club speed.

Dynamic weight shift. Increasing momentum, power and speed.

(4) Hands- Faster in transition. Creates more **kinetic energy** / speed on the downswing.

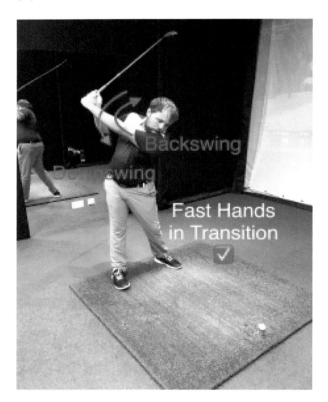

Neck down limits a golfer's shoulder turn.

See influence 2 - Transition page 173.

This does need to be checked at Set Up.

Neck Down Restricts Shoulder Turn

Neck Up / Level Allows Shoulders to Turn More Freely

Increase Club Speed:

Impact - Faults and Fixes:

Dominant Influences:

(1) Hands- speed. Faster hands = faster club speed.

(2) Elbows- trail extending. Gives more "width." Think: Trail elbow extends out before impact

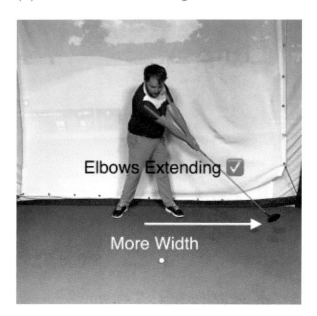

(3) Torso & pelvis- **The speed in which you "rotate" can contribute to club speed.**

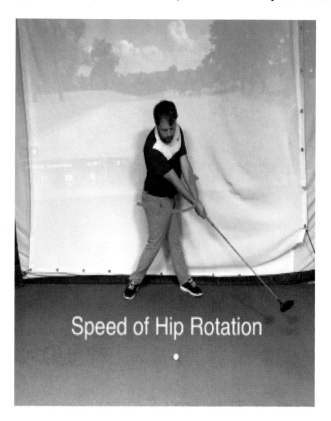

(4) Wrists- Lead wrist bowed. ***Explanation below pictures**

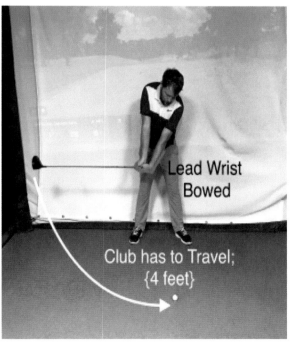

PICTURE LEFT = Hands by pocket, club has to travel 2 feet to golf ball.

PICTURE RIGHT = Hands by pocket, club has to travel 4 feet to golf ball.

Although the hand distance is the same, the club distance is further = faster release & "lag."

Conclusions and Remarks

On this Book:

It has been challenging. There have been moments where I have felt like banging my head against the desk.

Repeatedly!

Trying to get my head around how each Range of Motion effects every single shot type, well…. Pffftttttt.

I'll stop there, before I leave an imprint in the woodwork.

As I type this, I'm not sure if I will get it published. (I'm a golf coach, not an author). How do you publish a book???

Worst case - I'm a much more informed golf coach going forward.

On Golf:

The more I study the game, the more I believe this:

There is no perfect golf swing. Only the idea of a perfect golf swing. And even that 'perfect swing,' isn't 'perfect' for everyone.

We are different shapes; different sizes and our bodies have different ranges of mobility.

Take my hypothetical example as a golf coach:

09.00 lesson = 15-year-old gymnast.

10.00 lesson = 75-year-old with a bad back.

If I'm coaching a perfect method, then these two golfers' swings should look the same?????

On Swing Changes:

The problem I see and have experienced personally, is:

We buy into the idea that to "be a good golfer" or "to get better" we need to swing it a certain way, e.g., on plane.

As I understand golf more, I watch the guys on TV (the guys earning millions in prize money because of their ability) and I see all sorts of different swings. All sorts of different set ups. Different ball flights, grips, wrist positions etc. But… These guys have "found a way that works for them."

If there is a perfect swing, then why do the top 50 players in the world all look so different???

As I type this now 4 weeks ago Bryson DeChambeau won the 2020 Us Open and Matt Wolf came 2nd. You couldn't get two more "unorthodox" golfers.

What's the Answer Then:

What I do believe we should try to achieve is: **PIP.**

PERFECT IMPACT, PERSONALLY.

Personally, being the operative word:

If a *drawer* of the ball, wants to achieve a good impact position. Their impact factors have to be completely different, from the golfer who *fades* the ball.

The Question on Page 13 –

Should you optimise your set up?

I believe we should. But we often cringe at the thought of having an unorthodox, or "a weird" set up. Why... If it's going to make us better golfers???

The answer is likely linked to *'the search for the perfect swing:'*

Sadly. For a lot of us. (myself included) It's possibly rooted in insecurity and vanity. *Not for everyone, but for some of us:*

*W*e care more about the way our swings look, or worse (yet closer to the truth), more about what people think, about the way our swings look.

It could be said that:

"We are placing more emphasis on looking good, than playing good."

LET ME BE CLEAR:

I'm not saying you shouldn't make swing changes!!! But you shouldn't make swing changes just to 'look better.'

You should make swing changes to 'perform better.'

TO THE GOLFER AND NOT THE GOLF COACH:

If you want to get *more enjoyment* out of golf, learn to love *your* game. Embrace *your* style.

Love *your* swing.

NOW:

If you've got the shanks, it's going to be difficult to love that!!!!

You're obviously hitting the heel... A LOT!!!

But you don't need to be so critical of yourself.

You just need to move the strike an inch closer to the centre of the club face.

Simple right???

Not rebuild your entire swing.

(It will just feel unnatural)

One final truth before I love and leave you:

"How," is not as important, as "How Many."

Printed in Great Britain
by Amazon